Merlin The Magician

Merlin

Merlin stood upon the moors and read signs in the fog that hovered just inches above the ground. In the panorama before him, the great wizard saw that Briton was heavily burdened by destiny. Arthur would not remain king forever, and there were those who wanted him removed from the throne before Fortune had a chance to make her final spin upon the wheel.

Life had been much more simple in the Old Age, in the days when treachery did not slither so freely throughout Breton. Merlin manifested himself into the past and stood upon the hills of Northern Briton to watch visions of his youth play before his eyes.

Northumbria buckled against the mighty blasts of Boreas. Forest trees splintered; mountains cracked and toppled; rivers ran dry. Yet, above the bellowing rage of the holocaust, Merlin heard the terrified screams of his young mother. Within the swirls of a distant mist, he watched her struggle against the powerful arms and burning lust of a demon. The virgin was no match and the demon snatched her up in his arms and took the girl against her will. Three moons later Merlin stood atop the Northumbrian hills and gazed upon his own birth.

In those dark and desperate ages, unwed mothers were thought to be the temptresses of the devil and were burned or drowned as witches. Merlin's young mother hid herself and traveled by night across the wilderness with a newborn son cradled in her arms. But she was found and tried for her sin in the court of Blaise. Merlin again spoke the words that he had used when only 18 months old, and again he won his mother's freedom with arguments of logic and reason.

Several seasons later the great wizard felt the arms of Vortigern's guard upon him as the soldiers wrestled him to the ground before the ruin of a decrepit castle. The King had commanded that a fatherless child be sacrificed to break the enchantment that toppled the walls of his castle. And again Merlin spoke the words of his youth.

"Stand to and dig at the center of the foundation." Fire burned in his eyes and smoke billowed from his mouth as Merlin commanded Vortigern's men. "There, at the center of your troubles, you will find a sleeping dragon, and thus the reason why your castle walls will not stand."

The soldiers dug and killed the dragon that they found buried, sleeping in the belly of the earth.

The Dragon's Breath. Merlin had used it many times in the past to secure a heritage for the grand lands of Briton. He had used it to conceal the identity of Uther Pendragon so that the king could march into Cornwall and lay with the duke's wife, Igrayne. Merlin demanded the product of the king's lust as payment for his part in the deed and spirited the newborn to the woods until the boy came of age and was crowned King of Briton.

Merlin carried himself back to the present and stood upon a hill that overlooked Camelot. His heart fell heavy with sorrow. Nothing within his power could save Arthur from the evil clutches of Morgan le Fay. The king's sister was a powerful sorceress in her own right; her magic was empowered by the Realm of Water. Merlin was empowered by the earth, and to mingle earth enchantments with spells of the water would cast the world into inconceivable darkness. The mighty wizard could only counsel Arthur against dangerous paths and choices. And yet, even his counsel began to lack authority.

Arthur paid little heed to the wizard's reproach against marriage. The king had his eyes set upon Guinevere, the lovely maiden of Leondegrance. Yes, she was beautiful, but Merlin cast his eyes upon the future and saw that Guinevere's heart belonged to another man and that she would break the king's heart two-fold and shatter the foundation of Arthur's sovereignty. Morgan le Fay would take hold of the cracks in Camelot and rip Briton asunder.

Merlin saw his own death upon the guise of the future. He had fallen in love with the Lady of the Lake and against his own better judgment, paid little heed to the augury of the approaching winter. He made love to his mistress beneath the trees of Northumbria and bathed with her in waters of the Highland Valleys. But the future harbored death. The ancient sage watched as his love tempted his pride and enticed him to reveal his knowledge of the mystical world. And on a day as dark as the Apochryphia, he watched in helplessness as the lady locked him away forever in the confines of a huge rock.

Merlin sat down upon the mountain above Camelot and wailed with the sounds of primal eternity.

Arthur

A cool March mist floated gently across the hills of Wincester. Nobles, knights and peasants alike stood in a circle to watch a boy take his turn at the sword in the stone. He was but 17, a bit thin and common, yet his forearms and shoulders were thick. His eyes glowed with pride, his countenance marked with a noble steadiness. And with sudden determination, he gripped the hilt of the Sword of Kings amid the anxious gasps of the Breton people. The sword was free. Arthur stood in victory, emblazoned with light of heaven, his right arm thrusting the sacred sword toward the clouds. It mattered little that he was a boy. Breton at last had a King.

And Arthur was a good king. He ruled with the fairness of heaven and the logic of the ages. To honor the valiant men who fought beside him to secure the safety of Breton from Saxon invaders, and even the brave men who yielded to his sword, King Arthur established the order of the Knights of the Round Table and offered all worthy knights a fellowship at the court of Camelot. The Breton people, united and free, enjoyed prosperity and fulfillment in the fertile land of their ancient fathers.

Yet, even the most magnificent of gardens harbors a snake. Fortune spins her wheel in accordance to her own will and Arthur found himself caught within an unending cycle of treachery and treason, beleaguered by the evil schemes and enchantments of his sorceress sister, Morgan le Fay.

On a night as black as the adder's breath, Morgan crept to the walls of Camelot and camped near the fortress gate. She scurried in mad circles around her small fire and wove a web of bitter enchantment in the rising swirls of smoke. Morgan devoted her entire life to a single purpose — the death of her brother, Arthur, King of the Britons.

Arthur, unaware of his sister's intent, committed himself to the land and its people. But most of all, he rode alongside his knights in quest of honorable deeds and challenges. It happened upon a summer day that he and Sir Bors, while hunting the White Hart, chanced upon a small lodging boat moored upon the banks of the Royal River. The vessel was decorated with sails of fine crimson silk, the rigging woven from strings of pearl and the prow carved of the finest northern ash. Arthur dismounted his steed and stepped to the river bank to inspect the beautiful craftsmanship of the glimmering boat. But as he reached out his right hand to touch the prow, he found himself ensnared in the grip of magic and bound by shackles in the bowels of a cavernous dungeon.

Knights from all the past Ages of Man lay moaning and writhing in pain upon the muddy floor of the giant prison cell. Bodies of the dead and dying were strewn about the moldy corners. Arthur gripped the bars of the only window and yelled for his release.

"Save your strength," came a whisper from the darkest corner of the cell. A man hobbled over the sick and dying knights and stepped into the dim light of the window. "You are the only one who can save yourself, and those of us who still live if you so choose."

Arthur put his arms around the knight's shoulders to support the man as they talked. "How may I do so?" asked Arthur.

"The queen of this castle decreed that no man shall be released from the bounds of this dungeon until one among us can defeat her unbeaten champion."

"And how can I meet this knight?" Arthur helped the old man onto a rotted, wooden stool beneath the window. "Tell me. How can I win our release?"

The old man sighed with despair. "All you need do is accept the challenge."

Arthur stood tall, chin up and shoulders thrown back with pride. "I so choose."

In a flash of crimson light, Arthur found himself upon a battlefield. A knight in gold armor stood but ten paces off. A pavilion, within a stone's throw from the knights, sheltered a veiled queen from the heat of the noonday sun. She raised her left hand and motioned for Arthur to step forward and choose a weapon of his liking. Arthur ignored the offer and reached to his side for Excalibur, but he found nothing upon his hip. He was struck with fear for a moment as he frantically searched with his eyes across the field. And then he found it. The sword Excalibur, given to him by the Lady of the Lake, rested in the hands of his adversary.

The knight lunged mercilessly at Arthur, striking the king with shattering blows that would have felled a lesser man. Arthur parlayed with a lance, yet he could not avoid the attacks of his enemy. The golden knight buffeted Arthur solidly upon the helm. The king dropped to his knees. Bleeding from many dangerous wounds, Arthur prepared himself for death. But as the knight stepped forward to drop the final blow, Arthur summoned all of his remaining strength and upended his surprised foe. Excalibur came free, flew several yards into the air and stuck in the ground near its rightful owner. Arthur secured the hilt of the familiar weapon in his hand and raised it above his head. The mighty sword roared like thunder as it sliced through the air and cleaved the knight in two at his midsection. The battlefield was thrown into immediate panic. Arthur ran to the edge of the forest where the pavilion once stood, but all had fled at the sight of their defeated champion.

Only the queen remained. She stopped her horse under cover of the shadows and the thicket and sat motionless upon the saddle. Arthur gazed at her, sensing that he had seen her bewitching eyes within the keep of Camelot. The queen dropped her veil and then raised up her hands to reveal the scabbard of Excalibur, a sheath of enchantment more powerful than the sword itself. And with a hideous cackle, Morgan le Fay rode off through the wilderness to plot another scheme.

Arthur had regained possession of the sword and, for the moment, cared little for the scabbard. His thoughts were too distracted by the horror that he had discovered. Upon one knee, the King of the Britons cried out against the villainous, evil nature of his own sister.

Merlin Overlay

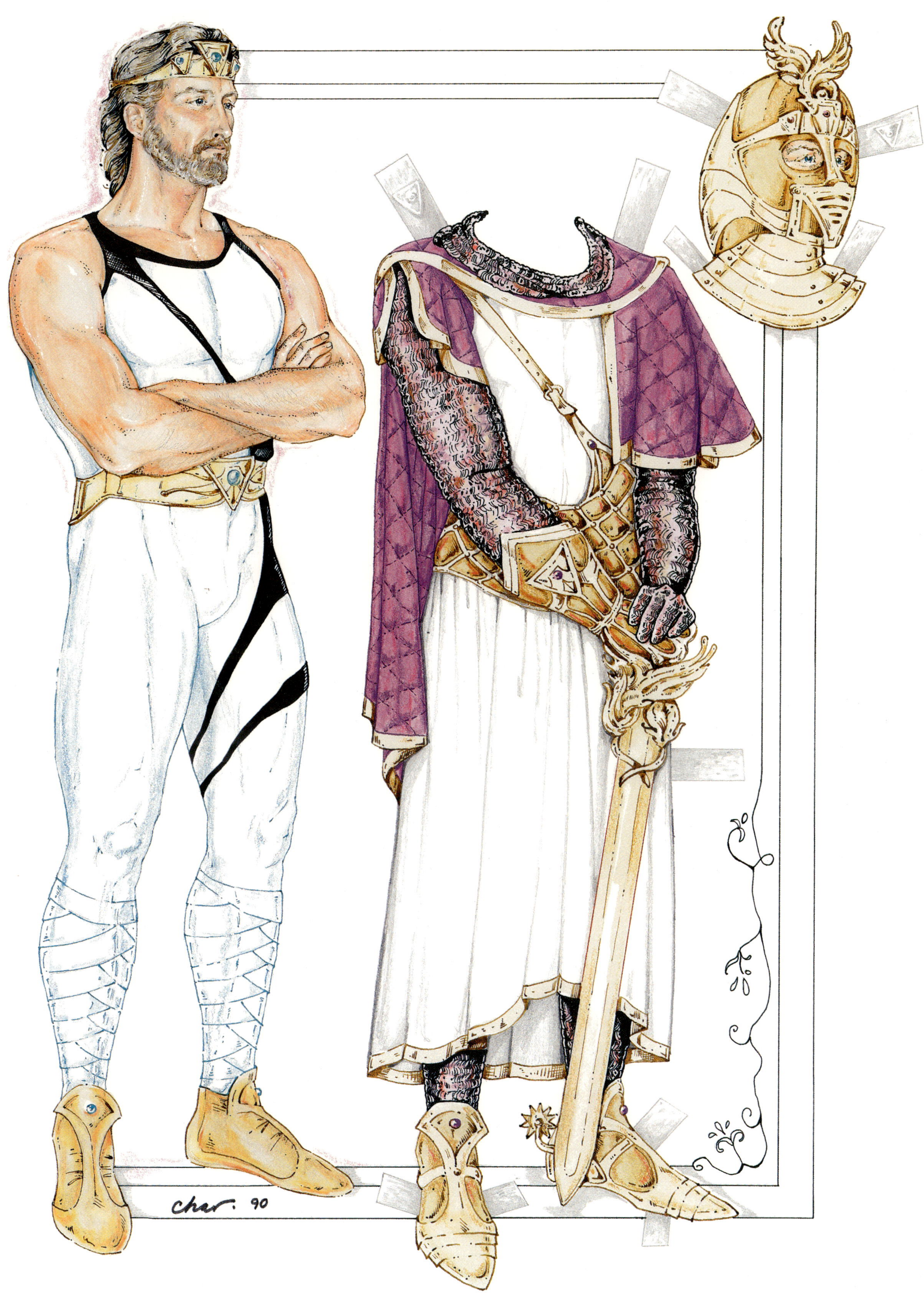

King Arthur

Guinevere

Upon her head she wore a garland of clover, a delicate crown of beauty that shimmered against the blackness of her hair. Her eyes sparkled with starlight, radiated the whiteness of her satin skin and burned into the hearts of every man who walked the fertile valleys of Breton. Her name was Guinevere, Arthur's queen. At night, when the moon floated in fullness across the midnight sky, she loved her king with the intense passion of a lioness. Yet, as she sat beside her window and listened to the morning breeze sing through the leaves of the hawthorne trees, Guinevere's heart would whisper a silent longing for another man.

She was young and the pomp and pageantry of Camelot reeled her senses. She enjoyed her position, the responsibilities and duties required of the king's wife, and she bathed in the attention given to her by the knights of Arthur's court. But one knight above all others had taken command of her heart. His name was Lancelot, the most revered knight in all Breton, the king's best friend and appointed champion of the queen. By her own secret command, Guinevere appointed Lancelot as the champion of her love. She tried to conceal her desire, but there were those in Camelot who sensed the queen's adulterous passion and plotted to use it for their own ambitions.

Mordred waited and watched in the shadows of Camelot, hoping to discover an indiscretion of the queen that would assist his mother in the overthrow of Arthur's rule in Briton. Every night he stole away to the woods and reported Guinevere's activities to Morgan le Fay, and together the evil souls plotted against the trust that Arthur held in his queen.

On the eve after Harvest, Guinevere laid out a noble feast of meats and fruits and invited the knights of the Round Table to dine with her upon the prosperity of Briton. Camelot reveled in the feast. But Sir Patrice plucked a pear from the center of a basket and went mad at the first bite of the poisoned fruit. He roared in anguish across the Feasting Hall, pulled out his own hair and plucked out his eyes, and then fell dead upon the floor. The knights of the fellowship wailed in agony over the death of their beloved brother. And all present pointed toward Guinevere and accused her of murder.

Morgan le Fay sat upon her throne in the bowels of the earth and cackled with impertinent satisfaction.

Arthur had no choice but to commit his queen to a Trial by Fire. Thirty knights had witnessed Patrice's death at the fatal feast and all accused Guinevere of having placed a poison pear upon the table. Breton law dictated that any person accused of such a heinous crime by so many must stand judgment before God. And so, with heavy heart, Arthur commanded that his queen be bound to a wooden stake and set aflame. If innocent of Patrice's death, Guinevere would survive the fire, if guilty, the lovely queen of Camelot would burn to ashes.

Lancelot was reported to be riding in the outlands, too distant to come forward and champion the queen. Yet all eyes glanced toward the horizon in hope that the Silver Knight would appear and rescue her, for there was not one knight of the fellowship who dared take up Guinevere's cause. Too many had witnessed the horror at the feast, and though they loved their queen they sensed that any attempt to save her would be futile. God would surely strike down any man who defended a murderess.

The fire was kindled. Smoke stung Guinevere's eyes and slithered through her hair. The scorched smell of impending death hung upon the chilly breeze. All who stood to watch the judgment of the queen wept for the horror that would soon blacken the once beautiful landscape of Briton.

But a silhouette appeared on the horizon, a horse of great speed that carried a tall rider. Lancelot had come. He dismounted his horse, stepped into the flames that roared around his secret lover and hacked with all his strength at the ropes that bound her hands. Rain fell from the clouds and hissed as it struck the fire. Lightning creased the sky and shattered upon the earth as Lancelot raised his sword to severe the last knot that held Guinevere to the stake. Amidst a blinding flash of light, Lancelot stepped forward and delivered his queen into the joyful arms of Arthur.

"She is innocent, my lord." Lancelot gasped with fatigue as he spoke. "I have proven her loyalty and virtue this day, for neither the fire or the lightning touched me as I rescued her from a grisly fate."

Morgan le Fay was the only soul in Breton who did not rejoice in the renewed vigor of the land. She sat upon her throne and chanted incantations toward the future.

Lancelot and Guinevere

Beltane fires flickered in the breath of spring. The maidens of Camelot danced around the Maypoles while their anxious suitors sang the songs of Bacchus. Only one room in the Kingdom remained untouched by the gaiety of the new season.

Guinevere sat in the window of her chamber and gazed in melancholy toward the North Star. She wrestled with her thoughts of deceit but could no longer defend herself from the adulterous passions that burned in her heart. Guinevere loved Lancelot, and she did not want to live if she could not bathe in the love of her noble champion.

Lancelot took refuge in the Breton forests, yet he could not hide from the desire that swelled within him like an overflowing fountain. He was the queen's champion, bound by a vow of chivalry to defend her honor and virtue. To hold her in his arms he must break his sacred oath and place her reputation in dire jeopardy. But he could no longer control his dangerous passion.

Beneath the glow of a waning moon, Lancelot ran the secret paths of the ancient forest toward Camelot. Quietly, he stole his way through the castle gate, climbed the stone wall of the keep and stepped into the candlelight of Guinevere's chamber. The queen stood in the center of the room, dressed in a white robe with a necklace strung from roses and purple lilies. Lancelot dropped to one knee.

"Forgive me, my queen, but I can no longer control my desire."

She turned to face the knight. "Will you love me?"

"With all my heart and soul."

Guinevere rushed into Lancelot's arms. The lovers fell upon the bed with burning passion.

Morning came. Lancelot and Guinevere failed to rise with the sun. Mordred, who had snuck to the queen's door and overheard her indiscretion, rallied a group of fellow knights and stationed himself outside the queen's chamber. At the first sound of stirring within, the dark prince burst through the door and challenged Lancelot and Guinevere to defend themselves of their treasonous impropriety. Lancelot, realizing that he could not fight off Mordred and the approaching knights, leaped out the chamber window and fled into the forest.

Arthur was summoned to the queen's chamber. He stepped into the room and immediately wept. Guinevere remained silent. She knew that nothing she said could wash away the stain of treason and adultery that she had brought upon Briton.

The following morning Arthur commanded that his five best knights escort the queen into the outlying hills and execute her. Gawain took charge of the guard and wept when he ordered that Guinevere be bound in an ox-cart and driven to the top of Soul's Hill. But the queen's death procession was intercepted at the summit by a band of masked riders who engaged Arthur's knights in mortal combat. One of the marauders broke from the battle and released the queen from her bonds. Sir Gareth rushed toward the villain but was halted by a sword that skewered his body. The marauder doffed his mask and revealed himself as Lancelot. He cried for the death of his friend and silently commended Gareth's soul to heaven. And then, shouting an order for retreat above the clamor of engaged swords, Lancelot rode off with his lover.

Joyous Gard Castle rested far in the North, and for several days Lancelot and Guinevere basked in each other's embraces within the keep of the knight's sturdy fortress. But soon all joy was washed away by the danger of war. Arthur, upon news of Lancelot's latest treachery, called to arms and besieged Joyous Gard with a massive army. All of Breton wept as the two greatest friends of the ages fought against each other for the love of a woman.

Morgan le Fay howled with laughter at Breton's fatal misfortune.

Queen Guinevere

Sir Lancelot

Lancelot

The messenger collapsed upon the floor of the great hall. Sir Bors and Sir Gawain sprang from their seats at the Round Table and rushed to the old man's aid. The knights placed him in a chair and gave him a cup of wine. In his dying breaths, the old man spoke the message for which he had forded raging rivers, crossed treacherous lands and braved torrential rains to deliver:

> King Pelles had been maimed by a wound in his side that would not heal, and because of the king's infirmity the land had also fallen sick and had become a wasteland. Pelles's castle had begun to crumble and fall to the earth. Worse yet, Elaine, the king's beautiful daughter, was a captive in the highest tower of the disintegrating castle. Only the bravest and strongest knight of the Round Table could bring an end to the evil that afflicted King Pelles's kingdom.

When the old man spoke the last word of his dolorous message, he sank back into his chair — dead.

Lancelot jumped immediately from the Round Table and proclaimed himself champion of the cause. "I shall release King Pelles's lands from this evil, or else I shall die in my efforts." A cheer went up across the Round Table, and Lancelot strode off to make ready for his journey.

The morning was warm when Lancelot ventured forth on his task, and by afternoon the heat of the sun beat down hard upon the great knight's armor. Lancelot stopped to rest in the shade of a large apple tree and as he napped, he dreamed of a face. She was a princess, and if not for his devotion to Guinevere Lancelot would have sworn that the woman of his dream was the fairest damsel in all Breton. When he awoke, the knight realized that his dream was a sign, and he allowed the lingering image of the princess to lead him through a forest of disfigured and dying trees. At the far side of the crippled forest, Lancelot came upon a dark castle, its parapets shattered and its walls crumbling to the ground. The great knight from Camelot knew at once that he had reached his destination.

He dismounted his horse, but as he ran to search the tower for the imprisoned princess, the most fantastic creature that Lancelot had ever seen attacked from behind the crumbling walls. It was a dragon so huge that when it raised up on its hindquarters its head seemed to disappear into the clouds. The brave knight bared his sword and battled for hours with the fiery beast. Though the knight struck with all his might at the magnificent demon, he could not penetrate the armor of scales that protected the dragon's body. If the battle was to be won, the valiant knight would have to pierce the dragon's skull and lodge his sword in the beast's brain. Lancelot knew that the only way in which to reach the dragon's head was to jump from the top of the nearby tower. Avoiding several dangerous swipes of the dragon's enormous claws, Lancelot ducked into the tower and ascended the stairs to the highest chamber. The door to the room was encircled by fire, but Lancelot lowered his shoulder and broke through the barrier of heavy oak.

Inside the room Lancelot discovered the princess. She was chained to the inside of a large tub of boiling water. And though Elaine was silent, tears of incredible pain flowed down her cheeks. For the moment Lancelot forgot about the dragon and began to strike his sword on the chains that held Elaine in the scalding water. Stroke after stroke, Lancelot destroyed the tub and broke the bonds of the captive woman. Elaine rushed to her savior's arms, and at that moment a hideous shriek of agony issued from outside the tower. Lancelot and Elaine rushed to the window and saw the dragon engulfed with flames that shot skyward through thick billows of black smoke. Within moments, the only remains of the dragon were gray ashes and pieces of charred bone.

Lancelot's bravery and his rescue of Elaine of Pelles broke the evil spell that gripped the kingdom. And though the king still suffered from the wound in his side that would not heal, he commanded that a celebration be held in Lancelot's honor that very night.

King Pelles knew of the prophecy that told of the birth of the greatest knight in the world, and he also knew that Lancelot would be the father of that wonderful knight. And so, with the help of his court enchantress, King Pelles devised a way in which his daughter, Elaine, would be the mother of that child.

That night, while the princess slept, the enchantress crept into the chamber and transformed Elaine into the visage of Queen Guinevere and instructed her to visit the chamber of Lancelot. The knight woke suddenly and could not believe his eyes. Standing before his bed was a woman whom he thought to be Guinevere, Queen of Camelot, the woman he cherished above all others in the world. Without speaking, Lancelot took his lover into his arms and embraced her through the night.

Morning brought disaster. Lancelot woke and discovered that the woman with whom he had lain was not the queen. It had been Elaine, King Pelles's daughter. Overcome with guilt, the knight threw himself against the walls of the room, clawed at his own face and tore at his hair. Elaine tried to comfort him, but Lancelot accused her of conjuring the trickery against him and would not allow her help. In his outrage, the distraught knight threw himself from the chamber window and disappeared into the forest.

For two years Lancelot wandered in madness through the dark woods of Briton.

Elaine gave birth to a son and named the child Galahad, the Knight of Peace.

Elaine le Blank

Elaine le Blank stood in the hallway of her father's castle and gazed into the light of the world. Never before had she seen such grace and nobility. And though she did not know the name of the knight who mesmerized her senses, she knew that she had fallen in love, and she knew that even to the ends of the earth she would follow her knight and offer him all the earthly comfort and joy he could ever desire.

The glorious knight traveled to the Celebration of Tournaments that King Arthur held in honor of Queen Guinevere. He needed lodgings so that he could rest before the morrow's jousts. Elaine waited by the side of her knight throughout the evening, offering him food and drink and her heavenly songs and verses.

By morning, Elaine's heart trembled with passion. The sweet princess knew that she would die if the knight refused to return and marry her. To show her love and to help speed him toward victory, Elaine offered the knight an embroidered red sleeve to mount upon his silver helm.

The knight went upon his way and bested every other knight who challenged him at the tournament. He was the victor of the field; yet in the heat of competition Sir Bors ran a truncheon through the body of the knight and leveled Elaine's champion upon the earth.

Elaine swooned at the sight of her shattered knight. Going without food and sleep, she tended to her champion's wounds and prayed every morning for his health. She fed him, comforted him and sang songs to cheer his spirit. Within a fortnight the knight's health improved and he prepared to leave the castle. His name was Lancelot. Elaine begged him to remain in Astolat and pleaded with him to marry her and live in the embrace of joyous love, but Lancelot's heart belonged to Guinevere. So he left the beautiful Elaine to her sorrow and tears.

The light of the world was gone. Elaine fell to her knees near death. She wrote a letter and then asked that her father place her body upon a bed of flowers within a small boat. She asked also that the boat be covered richly with black samite and that her body be dressed in her most beautiful white gown. In her hand she clutched the letter.

Sir Bernard obeyed his daughter's wishes and cast her floating bier down river to Camelot.

Everyone marveled at the beautiful boat that came to rest upon the shore. Yet when they found the beautiful princess, their hearts sank. The letter filled their eyes with tears.

"Dear Noble Knight, my Lancelot,
my Heart sang at first sight of you,
yet Death made wager with my Love,
though my Heart and Love were True.
And remind good Maidens that I was Pure,
and Loved only Sir Lancelot,
and Pray for me my Soul to keep,
your fair Maiden of Astolat."

Lady Elaine le Blank

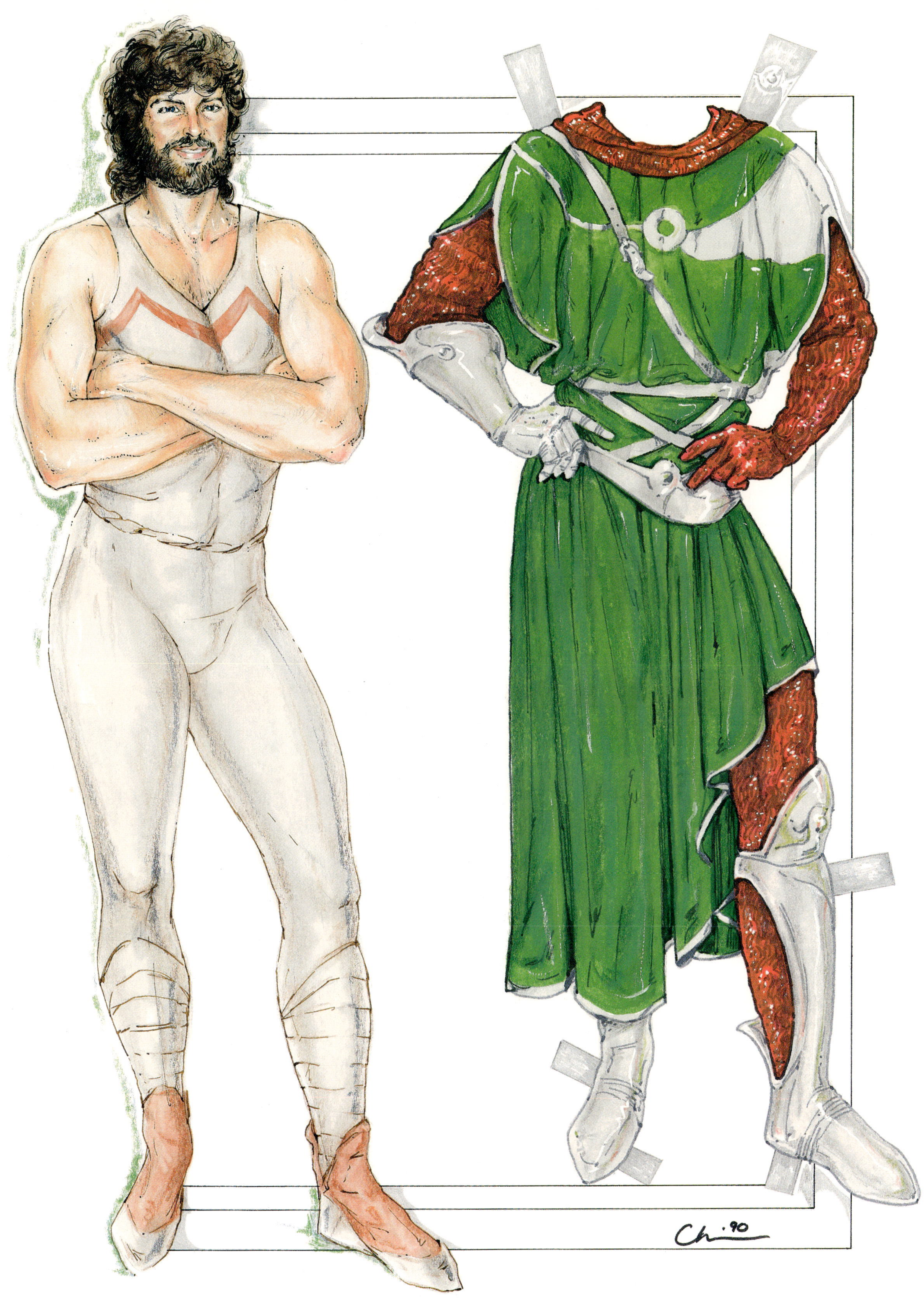

Sir Gawain

Gawain

As quick as lightning splinters a great oak, a flash of green light exploded in the royal hall, in the midst of which appeared an enormous green knight mounted upon the back of a horse that stood three heads taller than any man at Camelot. Arthur's knights froze in silence, each man afraid to approach the emerald specter.

The intruder was a giant, tall and sturdy like a sacred oak of the Druid Forest, dressed in a green shirt and trousers that had been stitched from leaves of fern and hawthorne. On his head he wore a crown of ivy.

"A lolly lot you have here, Arthur," the great knight sneered. "If I possessed a vicious manner, these men would be dead. Every one of them!"

Arthur bolted from his chair, glaring with disapproval at his knights as he marched forward to stand before the giant. "Who are you that dares interrupt our Yuletide celebration?"

The green knight dismounted his steed, his voice tinged with sarcasm. "Fear not, oh king of such brave knights. I come merely for sport." With a wave of his hand, the knight plucked a battle-ax from the air. "I will allow any man in this room one chance to remove my head from my shoulders. I ask only that whomsoever accepts the challenge will allow me a turn at his neck before the passing of next Yuletide."

No one stepped forward. Arthur spun on his heels and faced his cowering band of knights. "Since there be no man among you, I shall accept this challenge myself."

As Arthur reached for the ax, a voice called out near the back of the hall. "My king, no! It is unbecoming of you to take part in such vulgar folly. Let me accept the challenge." A young squire walked from the crowd of knights and stood before the king. "If you will make me a knight, I will gladly accept the challenge, if, when the man is dead, I am pardoned for committing such a grievous act of murder."

Arthur glanced around the room but found no one who volunteered to take the boy's place. Taking Excalibur from its sheath, the king raised the sword and made Gawain a knight. At the touch of the mighty sword, the young man took up the ax and severed the giant's head from his shoulders.

The green head rolled across the floor, and when it came to rest it fixed its eyes upon the shuddering lad. "A good stroke, young Gawain. I will expect to see you before next Yuletide." The body of the beheaded knight stepped over and picked the head up by the hair, and in another flash of green light, head, body and horse disappeared into the bitter winter.

The following morning Gawain mounted his horse and rode off through the four seasons in search of the Green Knight.

Winter had only begun, and the bitter snow and harsh winds gnawed at the knight's flesh and seeped into his blood. Spring offered little comfort. The rains that bring fertility to the land fell in torrents, rusted Gawain's armor and soaked through his clothes to cover his bones with an unceasing chill. The heat of the summer sun baked Gawain's flesh, and when the young knight discovered himself crawling through the dead leaves of autumn he began to doubt his strength and courage. In his heart he began to believe that he would fail in his quest and would die alone among unforgiving strangers.

Winter returned, and in a dying ember of hope the knight dragged himself to the door of a small hovel on the banks of a frozen river. Gawain knocked once and then collapsed.

found himself upon a down bed, a silk sheet tucked neatly beneath his battered arms. Golden rays of sunlight danced through an open window to his left, and from outside he heard the sweet song of a sparrow. Spring had come again, though the bright colors of the countryside beyond the window seemed distant and unreal.

From a door just beyond the foot of the bed a beautiful woman appeared. She wore a garland of ivy upon her straw-colored hair and a white dress that moved like a thin wisp of smoke on the gentle breeze. She carried a tray of fruit in her hands and, with an inviting smile, offered the fare to her guest.

For several days the routine continued. The woman brought Gawain breakfasts of fruit, lunches of biscuits and honey and in the evenings generous slices of beef and ham and crystal bottles of berry wine. Between meals, the woman remained in the room and sat beside Gawain. The young knight related his adventure with the Green Knight and his wearisome travels.

"But why have you caused yourself to suffer so?" asked the maiden. "Once you find the knight, he will only cut off your head." She looked at Gawain with sad eyes. "It seems a shame that a man such as you should so willingly seek his death."

"But perhaps I have avoided it," Gawain said happily as he pointed toward the window. But as he gazed through the open shutters, he saw bare oaks covered with snow.

The maiden stood solemnly beside the bed. "I am afraid, dear Gawain, that your life is not yet guaranteed, for this is Yuletide Eve and my husband, the knight of whom you speak, will return this evening to take his cut. And since in these few days I have come to love you, I offer myself for your last pleasure upon this earth." Her white gown dropped to the floor.

Gawain stared in wonder. Her beauty was beyond anything on earth. And yet, though his heart trembled with longing, he refused the woman and asked that she leave. At that moment the door of the room burst open and there stood the Green Knight.

"So, you have seen the pleasures of my wife."

Gawain shook his head and in a flurry sprang toward a corner near the bed and grabbed his sword.

"Fear not, Gawain. I know what has transpired here, and I commend your honor. I also commend your strength and bravery for having found me. Your travels were not easy."

Gawain stepped from behind the bed and confronted the knight. "Enough idle jabber," he said. "Take your cut and let's be done with it."

In silence, Gawain rested his head on the bed and awaited his doom. The Green Knight pulled his ax from the air, lifed it high and swung down with forceful speed. The blade whistled through the air and came to rest beside Gawain's head, just nicking the young knight's neck. Gawain jumped from the floor with his sword ready for battle. But as he turned, he watched the great knight wither before his eyes. The Green Knight, once a visage of great strength and might, melted into the form of an old man who gazed up with pleading eyes toward Gawain.

"Please do not stroke, gallant knight. You have proven yourself worthy of your knighthood, and in doing so I only hope that you have learned something about yourself and the ways of the world." The old man pulled an hourglass from the air, and as he turned it in his hands he fell to the ground and took the form of an infant. The woman took the child into her arms and walked out the door.

Gawain ran after her, but stopped abruptly as he cleared the threshold of the door. Once again he found himself alone, standing naked in a lush green forest beside a heap of rusted armor. In the far distance, he heard the cry of a baby.

Vivien
(Lady of the Lake)

In those days when Breton was still dark and Arthur fought to secure his rightful place as King of the Britons, the Lady of the Lake took a great interest in the affairs of men. She was amused by their childish naivete, their befuddled knowledge of nature and the world. In some respects, she looked upon humans as her children, a race of lost souls in desperate need of nurturing. And so it was, in those first moments of Arthur's march across the fertile mountains and valleys of Briton, that Vivien left her home beneath the waves of Loch Mar-Val and explored the world that men sought to conquer.

She whispered a message upon the cool breath of spring and asked that the wind carry it to a man called Merlin. And on an evening, as he stood in silent meditation before a giant oak in the Northumbrian forests, the great wizard heard the sound of Vivien's ancient voice. Wasting no time, Merlin whisked himself to Arthur's camp and bid the heir of Briton to follow. Arthur obeyed and in the morning found himself standing beside the thundering falls of a mighty river.

As the first rays of sun broke across a cloudless blue sky, the spray from the tumbling water began to shimmer like diamonds. The air seemed filled with precious jewels and gems. In the midst of a sparkling light, a beautiful woman rose from out of the water.

She carried a magnificent sword in her hands which she offered to Arthur. The young king graciously extended his arms and accepted the steel into his own hands. It was forged from the metal that can only be found in the Netherworld, a leather hilt adorned with inlaid gold and lapis lazuli and a tip so sharp that even heavy Roman armor shredded like thin parchment beneath its cut. It was the Sword of Kings, the sacred scimitar of Briton. Arthur raised Excalibur toward the sky and felt the glorious power of his ancestors race through his blood. With such a sword the young king knew that he was nearly invincible. And then, dropping to his knees in silent thanks and prayer, Arthur watched the Lady of the Lake fade into the cool spray of the waterfall.

But there was another gift which Vivien bestowed upon Arthur.

In her travels, the lady wandered to Gaul, a land besieged by Claudas and his Roman legions. Arthur offered his assistance, but for the moment was preoccupied with stabilizing his own lands and his throne. He could not arrive for many months. So King Ban rallied his countrymen to stand against Rome until Arthur arrived with the Breton army.

The Roman legions were strong, pushing the Gauls farther north until, at last, the women and children fled their homes and sought refuge on the western shores of Briton. In the exodus, King Ban's infant son was lost.

The Lady of the Lake found the child crying upon the bank of a small stream. He was a beautiful babe: deep blue eyes, golden hair, stronger and more stout than usual human infants of such a young age. Vivien knew that the babe was born of gentle birth and took him to her castle in the depths of Loch Mar-Val, where she suckled the infant from her own breast and bathed him in the crystal waters of her magical kingdom. Protected from the horrors that raged beyond the surface of his new home, the child grew strong and healthy. Vivien instructed him in the ways that she had observed of men, taught him to control his manner and speech and cautioned him to maintain a balance in his heart. She gave him lessons in the arts of chivalry and warfare and warned him about the dangers of love. On the boy's 16th birthday, she bestowed upon him a shining suit of silver armor and a sword that had been forged in the land of Faerie. She christened him with the name Lancelot of the Lake and, on a day when the sun covered the land with satin light, escorted the gallant knight to Camelot for him to seek fortune and glory in the service of King Arthur.

The Lady Of The Lake

Lady Of The Lake Overlay

The Lady and Her Children (Lady of the Lake)

Her mother was Danu, goddess mother of an ancient race called the Tuatha De' Danann, those people whom mortals collectively call Faerie. Her sister was Brigit, goddess of fire. Her brother Manannan was god of the sea. Her father was Great Dagda himself, God of All.

She was Vivien, the Lady of the Lake, protector of the land's sacred waters and keeper of the earth's most precious treasures. She lived beneath the waves of Mar-Val, a pristine lake that rested silently near the foot of a great mountain.

In those days when men were but new creatures upon the earth, fishermen used to row their boats across the smooth waters of Mar-Val. They caught large bounties of enormous silver and gold fish, which they eagerly shared with others of their kind in the mortal villages that bordered the shores of the magical lake. In the evenings, when the sun touched lightly upon the western rim of the world, the fishermen could see the sparkling pearl ramparts of Vivien's watery domain. And always, after a hearty and prosperous day, they would kneel in their boats and give thanks to the Lady for the generous gifts that she placed in their nets.

Upon the peaceful shores of Mar-Val, mortal children danced in the gentle waves and built glorious castles of sand. Sometimes the children pretended that they too were great fishermen like their fathers, and cast small nets made from string and yarn into the blue water. Vivien marveled at the beauty of mortal children and often placed fish in the crude nets woven by the small, innocent hands. During early mornings, when the fishermen were already embarked upon their daily journey, the Lady would stir a gentle breeze across the shore to sing harmonies with the happy songs of the children. Upon the surface of the lake she often lifted waterspouts that danced for hours to the sound of the small voices. On particular days, when the sun changed its course in the sky to signal the coming of a new season, the Lady of the Lake mounted a white stag and rode through the mortal villages, stopping frequently to play with the children upon the lakeshores. At night the Lady dreamed of the morrow when she would again bask in the beauty of those creatures that called themselves human.

But there came a time when the waves of Mar-Val were scorched with blood. Raiders came across the seas from the north and moved inland to the great mountain that overlooked the magical lake. The northern barbarians, clothed in the dark hides of grisly animals and armed with weapons of biting steel, killed the fishermen and the fishermen's wives. They burned the villages and the boats and bound the children in metal shackles to be taken away as slaves. In single file, and bound together by ropes knotted around their necks, the little children marched toward the sea and the boats that would carry them to a sorrowful fate. The sky echoed with their anguished cries.

The Lady of the Lake raged with anger at the death and destruction wrought upon her shores by the barbarians. She called upon her brother to sink the barbarian boats and strand the invaders on land, and then summoned the four winds to lock the murderers in the eye of a cyclone while she rescued the precious children stolen from her shores.

Knowing that their daughter would move swiftly in her rescue of the children, Dagda and Danu wasted no time in securing the earth against Vivien's anger. Danu collected the Tuatha and ushered them into a cave near the peak of the great mountain. Satisfied that all her people were entrenched in the security of the cave, Danu sealed the entrance and hid herself in the keep of her daughter's castle. Dagda burrowed deep underground and secured his grip upon the roots of the great oaks and ash to insure that the forests of the earth would not be swept away by his daughter's rage.

When the earth was anchored firmly in Dagda's grip and Danu's people were tucked safely away from the danger, Vivien unleashed her wrath.

Empowdered by her own anger and the forces of her kinsmen in nature, Lady of the Lake raised the waters of Mar-Val and flooded the earth. The heavens echoed with the roar of the water as it crested above the trees of the mythical forests and lapped angrily at the peak of the great mountain. The northern barbarians, locked in bitter combat with the four winds, glanced in terror at the sky and beheld the tumultuous wave that broke toward them. At the moment when the great wave exploded upon the dark raiders, the Lady of the Lake transformed her children. Their feet melted together and became magnificent golden flukes that tapered softly from their slender hips. Their hair became billowing silk. As Vivien's wrath washed across the face of the earth, the children propelled themselves to safety at the surface of the water.

Screaming and flailing their arms wildy in the water, the raiders were washed away to sea and drowned by Manannan.

When the waters subsided and Lake Mar-Val returned to its normal volume, Vivien discovered that her children had become separated. Some were stranded in the sea. Others were locked between the banks of the earth's rivers. A few remained in the waters of Mar-Val.

Yet Vivien did not morn the separation of her children. She had saved them from a doomed fate, and in joyous triumph she asked her kinsmen and the mother of earth to welcome the beautiful children and keep watch over their safety and freedom. Manannan smiled upon the new members of his family. He called them mermaids and took them into his own personal protection. The Earth Mother collected her children and dressed them in the comfort of her crystal streams, offering them sanctuary in glistening waterfalls and eddies. Vivien dressed her children in coats of white down and called them swans.

On summer evenings, when the warm sun blinks a last good-bye over the land, the children join their voices upon the gentle breeze and sing praise to their loving mother, the Lady of the Lake.

Tristram

Long ago, in the first Ages of Man, Ireland sorely defeated the Cornwall armies and demanded a yearly tribute. In the new age, King Mark refused to pay the tribute which had so long plagued his ancestors. And now, on the shores of a small island not half a league from the coast of Cornwall, Tristram came to champion his uncle's cause and rescue Cornwall from paying tribute to the Emerald Isle. He came to battle Marhaus, the champion of King Anguish and all Ireland, and the most feared knight in the world.

With a brave heart and a steady hand, the champion of Cornwall stepped onto the barren patch of sea-locked earth and faced his adversary.

"You are younger than I expected," bellowed Marhaus. "Perhaps you wish to commend your soul to heaven before we begin."

"I intend to leave this island alive," Tristram replied. With, that he charged at the great Irish knight.

The sun rose toward midday and still the battle raged. Tristram and Marhaus struck each other with blows that echoed like thunder above the heads of the distant onlookers. Blow after blow, the swords of the combatants clashed together, rocking the little island and causing the encircling water to ripple out toward the sea. By late afternoon, the Irish knight became tired.

"Perhaps your age has been to your advantage," Marhaus puffed. "I am not as young as I used to be, and I could stand a rest before we continue on through the night."

Though he felt not the least bit winded and would have continued to put up a diligent fight, Tristram agreed and lowered his sword. Marhaus, having tricked the younger knight into dropping his guard, lunged with his sword and pierced Tristram between the breastplate and his shoulder.

"And I am the victor!" hollered the great knight. "The tip of my sword is waxed with poison for which only my sister has the cure." He laughed defiantly in the face of his fallen foe.

Tristram, overwhelmed by rage that a knight of Marhaus's reputation would stoop to such treachery and deceit, raised his sword and brought it down square upon his enemy's helm. Tristram's sword broke in half as it ripped through the metal helmet and lodged itself in Marhaus's thick skull. "And now I am the victor!" Tristram bellowed, hoisting his sword toward the cheering crowd upon the far shore.

Feeling the poison in his veins, Tristram knew that he would die shortly if he did not seek out Marhaus's sister and receive the antidote. Also knowing that the maiden would never consent to heal her brother's killer, the young knight disguised himself as a minstrel and traveled to Ireland.

When he arrived at the court of King Anguish's castle, the maidens of Ireland became so entranced with the beautiful music of Tristram's harp that they gladly welcomed the young man into their company and asked him to play for them in the garden. Tristram told them that this would be impossible.

"In fighting for the love of a fair maiden," lamented Tristram, "I received a piercing wound from a poisoned sword. I fear that I will not live long enough to favor you with song."

One girl from the gathering of maidens stepped forward. She was the most beautiful of all. Her golden hair flowed like a waterfall in spring and her deep blue eyes radiated a warmth unequaled by the sun. She was the daughter of the king. Her name was Isolde. "I have something that may cure you," she said, taking the disguised knight by the hand." Isolde led Tristram to her own chamber and gave him an antidote for the poison that boiled in his blood.

In the days that followed Tristram and Isolde fell in love, and together they wandered the green hills and vibrant gardens that surrounded the castle. Tristram would play his harp and sing songs to describe the beauty of his lover. And always, Isolde would ask for more, just to hear the sweet voice of her cherished minstrel. But the day came when King Anguish discovered the identity of his daughter's lover and commanded that both of them appear in the royal hall.

Tristram held tight to the hands of his beautiful lover, knowing that the king would surely execute him and that he would never again gaze upon the lovely eyes of Isolde. But as Tristram entered the great hall, he noticed a demeanor upon the king that he did not expect, and as he and Isolde drew nearer to the Irish ruler the knight became confused as to the reason for his being summoned.

"I had intended to kill you when I first discovered who you are," King Anguish said. "But I have thought about it, and I realize that you were only doing what was necessary. Any man worth his armor would kill a charging adversary."

Isolde was horrified at her new discovery. She had not known that Tristram was her brother's killer. The princess gaped at her lover with wide, tearful eyes, and then buried her head in her hands and ran from the hall. Tristram wanted to follow her, but he knew that whatever comfort he could offer would be useless. Yes, he had killed the brother of the woman he loved. The dejected knight turned to face the king.

"I am most thankful for your pardon, my lord. Yet, I would gladly have died beneath Marhaus's sword to spare myself from seeing your daughter troubled with such grief." Tristram slumped before the king, as if in bitter defeat.

"You have gained much favor in my court, young knight, far more than you expected, perhaps." The king stood up from his royal chair. "I respect your strength and your courage, particularly in seeking help in a country from which you surely must have expected grave hostility once your identity was known. But I release you from my custody, brave Tristram, and I think it best that you leave Ireland altogether."

Tristram glanced toward the door where Isolde had fled and then turned back to the king. "Sire, your leniency is more than generous and your advice is wise. If there is a time when the fair Isolde does not cringe at the sound of my name, would you extend my affections?"

King Anguish nodded and watched the sad knight walk from the castle.

Sir Tristram

La Belle Isolde

Tristram and Isolde

Tristram stood upon the prow of the boat that sailed him home. The sea was calm and the sky clear, yet the knight did not see the beauty of the world that surrounded him. A stormy heart clouded Tristram's thoughts. The only thing that he could see or think about was the lovely Isolde. He had held her in his arms, had kissed her cheeks a thousand times, and then he lost her. Tristram's heart weighed heavy as he disembarked from the boat and returned to Tintagel Castle.

The return to Cornwall was not what Tristram expected. His uncle seemed cold and distant. A group of knights who were jealous of Tristram's handsomeness and strength tried to increase their own position in the castle by slandering the good knight's name all across Cornwall, and King Mark listened. But the king also listened to the stories that his nephew told of Isolde, and for that reason only he allowed Tristram to remain in the kingdom and sing songs that spoke of the most precious gem on Emerald Isle.

On one warm spring day King Mark became so overwhelmed with a particular song of Isolde's beauty that he summonded Tristram to appear in the royal chamber.

"Nephew, the songs that you sing of the Irish princess have stolen my heart. I want you to sail to King Anguish and ask for his daughter's hand. I should like to marry her on the first day of summer."

Tristram nodded, but upon returning to his own chamber, fell to his knees and wept. He had hoped one day to regain the favor of the princess, but it would be impossible if she was the bride of King Mark.

Isolde sat by her window and stared across the ocean that led to Cornwall. She had long since forgiven Tristram for killing her brother. It was as her father had said: A brave knight only does what he has to do. And the love that the gallant knight had kindled in her heart was too strong to ignore.

Every morning the princess waited by her window, ate little and avoided her daily walks through the gardens with the other maidens of the castle. She waited and watched, hoping that someday her love would return.

On one beautiful morning, while birds twittered among the cherry blossoms and golden sunlight danced upon the leaves of budding roses and carnations, Isolde spied a sail on the horizon, trimmed in gold with the bold emblem of Cornwall embroidered at its center. Isolde's heart sang, and the maiden ran to the shore to see what news she could discover about her lost love. Her heart nearly fluttered away with excitement at the sight of Tristram standing on the prow. The boat landed and Tristram stepped again upon the green soil of Ireland. Isolde rushed into her lover's arms and would not let him go. They remained on the shore for a long time, holding and kissing each other, and professing their undying love.

That afternoon, in a garden behind the castle, Tristram was taken to see the king. Anguish greeted the knight with open arms and ordered that a feast be prepared to honor the noble guest. The king and his daughter escorted Tristram around the court and pointed out the new shrubs and flowers that had come from exotic places. But as evening fell, the joyous reunion came to an end.

"Why have you come back to Ireland, Sir Tristram?" King Anguish asked.

The knight's heart sank. Until now he had forgotten the reason for his return. He could not bear to look at Isolde, and his words stumbled across his lips as he spoke his business. "I have come on behalf of my uncle, King Mark of Cornwall. It is his desire to seal his and Ireland's kingdom together. And to do so he asks for the hand of Princess Isolde in marriage."

Isolde staggered at the pronouncement of the proposal. For a fleeting moment she thought that Tristram would be the bond between the two kingdoms, but the smile that sparked across her face suddenly fell to sadness. Her dreams of living forever in the arms of her loving knight vanished upon a cool, evening breeze.

King Anguish gazed hard at Tristram. "And how do you feel about the union, sir knight?"

"I am sworn to obey my uncle's commands and to further whatever cause he deems necessary for the prosperity of Cornwall."

"Indeed. This would also be a good cause for Ireland," the king said in a serious tone. "I had thought perhaps that there would be another match for my daughter, but this one is not to my disliking." His eyes were thoughtful, yet stern as he gazed toward his daughter. "We are all born to a purpose, and I hope my daugher will understand the purpose for which she can best help Ireland. I will grant King Mark's request."

Isolde did understand her purpose. As a princess it was her duty to do whatever was best for the kingdom, even if that duty filled her heart with sorrow. Tristram also understood, and in solemn resignation took the hand of the beautiful princess and walked one last time across the Irish hillside.

A boat was prepared the following morning. Tristram took his place at the prow and escorted fair Isolde and her maidens to the shores of Cornwall. A Cornish royal guard met the boat, and Isolde arrived at the court of Tintagel in the midst of a grand procession. King Mark met his bride at the castle gate and, staggered by the princess's illustrious beauty, set an immediate date for the wedding. Before showing Isolde around the castle, King Mark stepped over to Tristram.

"Nephew, you have performed your duties well. I do fear, however, that the love between you and I has diminished, and I ask that you leave Cornwall, never to return."

Tristram was shattered. Though Isolde was to be another man's wife, he had hoped that being able to see her walk among the Cornish gardens and skip barefoot across the sandy shoreline would at least ease some of the pain in his heart. But his uncle's intentions were clear, and Tristram decided to obey them.

He made up his mind to travel to Camelot and seek a position in the service of King Arthur. But before leaving upon his journey, Tristram desired to see his love one last time.

Waiting until nightfall, the knight scaled the wall of the castle and entered through the window of Isolde's chamber. The princess was there, and she ran to the arms of her secret lover. They kissed each other through their tears, and with warm embraces consoled each other of their predicament. But in their sorrowful passion, they failed to hear the door of the chamber.

King Mark crept quietly into his bride's room, holding back his boiling anger as he watched the lovers embrace. Without a sound, he stepped behind his nephew. Isolde screamed but it was too late. King Mark raised a silver dagger and slammed it into Tristram's back. The valiant knight slipped from his lover's arms. He was dead.

Isolde screamed with sorrow and hate, tears streaming down her cheeks as she clawed her fingers across the murderous king's face, but her anger quickly gave way again to sorrow. The princess dropped to her knees beside the fallen knight. And then, with a fatal saddened scream, she pulled the knife from Tristram's back and plunged it into her own broken heart.

King Mark gazed in horror toward the dead lovers at his feet.

Morgan le Fay

Gentle rains fell from a soft white sky. A delicate mist wafted lightly across the vibrant leaves of hawthorne and petals of succulent lilac. The emerald forest of Avalon breathed with new life. A tender silence rose through the trees and enveloped the bright but sunless sky in warmth and comfort.

Morgana stepped from the ephemeral waters of the enchanted island, naked and beautiful, her long red hair caressed gently by an easy breeze, her amethyst eyes burning with the power of an ancient magic. She was the protector of the earth's waters and daughter to the Lady of the Lake. Even the great gods of the far north could not resist Morgana's empyrean seductions and often found themselves willingly caught in her Nirvanic embraces, an experience that they did not regret. But to mortal men she was Morgan le Fay, a dangerous temptress, unrivaled as a sensuous lover, yet more treacherous than a crimson adder. Any knight who yielded to Morgan's passionate fire woke the following morning in the chains of impending death.

In the softness of morning, Morgan drifted across the waters of Avalon and stepped quietly through the mortal forests of Breton, stopping occasionally to shower in the gentle rains that brought a prosperous fertility upon the land. When she reached the edge of the Briton Forest, she stopped and gazed upon the mighty fortress of Camelot. Sunlight broke through the clouds and reflected brightly from the golden walls of the castle. It was a beautiful morning. It was a good day for murder.

Morgan hated her brother. At the expense of her father's life, Arthur inherited the great land called Briton. The crown should have gone to Morgan, but women were not allowed to rule in the place of men. And in her bitterness and anger, the enchantress set about to kill King Arthur, the half-brother that had stolen her claim to the throne.

She sat upon the soft ground of the forest and wove herself a silk dress from spiderwebs which she carefully plucked from the branches of sacred oaks. When the sun finally drifted lazily below the horizon and the moonlight disappeared behind fangs of thundering clouds, Morgan dressed herself in the mystical gown and walked to the gates of Camelot.

Briton was at peace with the world and had been since that time when Arthur secured his place upon the throne. Morgan found it easy to slip unseen past the meager guards who stood at the gate. Making her way quietly into the King's great hall, the daughter of Vivien stopped at the base of the tower stairs and listened for the sounds of breathing. Her senses told her that her brother was in the chamber near the top of the tower. She ascended the stairs and stopped near Arthur's room. The door was ajar and she could see her brother upon his bed, studying several parchments that held his attention and kept his thoughts from suspecting the sinister plot that Morgan was about to unfold. In the dim torchlight of the hallway, the enchantress whispered an ancient incantation. She let the silk gown drop from her shoulders and hips and felt the soft tingle of magic weave its way around her sensual body. With light footsteps, she moved into her brother's chamber.

Arthur looked up from his papers and beheld the visage of his beautiful queen. Without a word, he motioned for her to come nearer. Morgan stepped to the bed and pressed herself against the king.

"My lord," she whispered, "I am here to soothe your weariness and calm your most passionate desires."

Ensnared by the beauty of the woman that lay before him, Arthur removed his armor and took the maiden in his strong arms. He kissed her gently upon the forehead and held her in his embrace until the morning. When he awoke, Arthur found himself alone and walking quietly down the hallway, found his queen asleep in her own chamber.

Outside, Morgan le Fay stood naked in the first light of morning, a fire of delight in her eyes. She carried inside her womb the seed of a boy. She would name him Mordred, and she would nurture the babe with her own breast and cradle it in her own arms. She would give the child all that he could possibly desire. And when the boy was grown, she would teach him the arts of warfare and offer him the throne of Briton. Mordred, the son of Arthur, would kill his father and take possession of the land.

Morgan laughed inwardly to herself. Once her son had wrested the throne from her brother, Briton would be plunged into chaos and darkness and her vengeance would be won.

Queen Morgan le Fay

Sir Mordred

Mordred

He was tall and strong, a favorite among the Breton damsels and esteemed by the knights of the Round Table as one of the most upright and chivalrous members of their order. By the grace of his father, Mordred was given command of several armies that went to Gaul to assist King Ban in his fight against Claudas. All of Camelot considered the king's mysterious son a boon to the kingdom.

No one but Morgan le Fay knew of the dark evil that boiled in the young knight's heart. He was intelligent and cunning, and able to shadow his true feelings and cover up his vicious deeds. It was he who delivered the pear that killed Sir Patrice and nearly cost Guinevere her life; and it was he who often disguised himself and ambushed unsuspecting knights riding through the Breton forests. Yes, Mordred was a demon, born in the fires of enchantment and nurtured by the vengeance that seethed throughout his mother's fiendish essence. Morgan le Fay existed only to exact revenge upon her brother, King Arthur. Mordred existed only to see that her wish came true. No mother could ever ask for a more devoted son.

The dark prince won his share of tournaments, profited more than enough from grateful people who offered him gifts as payment for gallant services that he performed for them. As he passed through the green countryside, the young maidens of Breton swooned and each vowed to be the one that captured the knight's heart, forcing him to break his vow of chastity.

But that was by day. In those hours when demonic creatures roam freely about the earth, Mordred visited the caverns of imps and devils who had kidnapped young women for the prince's vicious pleasure. And on those nights when the moon disappeared from the sky, Mordred would visit the hovel of his mother and plot continuing treachery against the king. So far, his plans had failed, and always it was Lancelot who rescued Guinevere, or even the king himself, from the devious clutches of Mordred's schemes. It was always Lancelot, and the dark prince decided to do away with the thorn in his paw.

Mordred was gifted with magical insight. He understood the ways of men, and he recognized the secret affection between Lancelot and the queen. He knew that, if given enough time and enough prodding, the queen and her beloved champion would no longer be able to control their passion and their desire for one another. Mordred knew that he could use Guinevere's impropriety against her, and in doing so could pit Lancelot and Arthur at each other's throat, and thus gain command of Briton.

Lurking in the shadows of moonlit trees, Mordred spied upon Lancelot and one night followed the great knight to the queen's private chamber. He leaned against the door and found the lovers trapped by the heat of their own passion. Mordred ran to the courtyard and assembled a band of knights, telling them that a villain had stolen into the queen's chamber and was preparing to kill her. The knights rushed boldly into Guinevere's chamber and caught the queen and her lover in a grievous act of treason. Lancelot escaped and fled from Camelot but the damage was done. The doomed fate of Briton was at hand and the death of Arthur was within Mordred's sinister grasp.

When word of Lancelot's and Guinevere's adultery reached Arthur, the king rallied his knights and ordered them to pursue the criminal that was once considered the greatest knight in Camelot. Arthur looked at his son. "You have proven yourself loyal to my kingdom," he said. "And in my absence I leave you to watch over my lands and protect the queen from anymore mischief." Arthur mounted his horse and rode off to fight the man who had stolen the heart of his wife.

Mordred howled at the moon and shook in a frenzy of laughter. The kingdom was his and when his father returned from his battles of jealous rage, the king would find himself ensnared by the bonds of death. It was a glorious night, a victorious night, and to celebrate, the traitorous prince rushed to Guinevere's chamber.

"I shall have you!" shouted Mordred, his voice almost insane. "And you shall be my queen. Thus shall my grip upon Breton be complete."

But Guinevere avoided the madman's advances and vowed that she would never submit to his vile wishes. Raging in anger, Mordred commanded that the queen be imprisoned in the darkest corner of the castle until such time when she felt compelled to drop on her knees and beg her new king for forgiveness. There were knights, however, that refused to obey the will of the usurper and, stealing quietly through the secret passages of Camelot, freed Guinevere and escorted her to the safety of a monastery in the south of Briton.

Mordred gathered an army of his loyal knights and set off after the escaped queen. Within a day's journey from the monastery, Mordred's assemblage reached the hills of the southern lands. They descended into a small valley, and rising over the far hill discovered Arthur's army lying in wait. The two kings stared at each other from the summits of opposite hills.

"As rightful king of the Britons, I have come to reclaim my lands. What say you, Mordred?"

The dark prince raised himself in the saddle and lofted his sword into the air. "You will not retake this land without the taste of steel."

No command was given; there was no need. Mordred's words were enough to signal the inevitable charge of the opposing armies. The banners of both legions snapped like hot flames in the cloudy sky. Swords and axes echoed like thunder as man fought against man. Blood soaked the ground and seemed to spread across the land like crimson paint upon a tattered canvas. A heavy rain did little to slow the frenzy of battle. Hundreds upon hundreds fell from their saddles and dropped dead upon the ground.

As evening approached and only a handful of men remained for either side, a father and son stood face-to-face at the center of the battlefield.

The rain beat against Arthur's face and mixed with the tears that flowed down his cheeks. "The treachery and doom that you have brought upon this land cannot be forgiven."

"I ask no forgiveness," Mordred hissed. "And at this moment I care nothing for this land or its people. My only desire is to see you dead."

Arthur glared at the demon before him and quietly whispered, "Then so be it, my son."

The two men lunged with their swords, piercing each other through the heart; in the driving rain they knelt together upon the muddy earth and studied the various hemispheres of death in one another's eyes.

Galahad

One seat remained vacant at the Round Table. Merlin had dubbed it the Siege Perilous because the chair was enchanted. Only the greatest knight in the world could take his seat upon the Siege Perilous. Several proud and boisterous knights had attempted to take a place on the chair, but each one died instantly upon sitting down. The knights of the Round Table begged Lancelot to take his place upon the Siege Perilous, but deep in his heart the Silver Knight knew that his secret love for Queen Guinevere would strike him dead if he dared sit on the chair. And so Siege Perilous remained vacant for many years.

On the eve of the Spring Equinox, as the knights of Camelot gathered together for a feast to celebrate the arrival of a new season, a stranger came to the kingdom. He was a monk named Nacians, and he brought a boy who desired to work in the service of King Arthur. Nacians escorted the boy around the table, instructing the lad to sit upon the Siege Perilous. The knights of the Round Table roared with discontent, but their objections were soon quelled by a magnificent sight. The boy lived as he sat upon the enchanted chair. The name Galahad etched itself in the wooden backrest. All the knights of the Round Table dropped to their knees to show their undying love and respect for the greatest knight in the world. Lancelot gazed in wonder at the strength and beauty of his fine son.

The following morning Galahad was made a knight by his father. The lad immediately asked Arthur's permission to go in search of the Holy Grail. Other knights asked the same, and the king granted permission to all, including Lancelot and Gawain, though Arthur knew that only Galahad would succeed.

Many knights died in their quest for the Holy Grail. The lands where they searched were treacherous and filled with unspoken danger. Errant knights were no match for the dire evils that ruled the distant lands. Only a handful of knights even came close to achieving the sacred chalice. Lancelot was among them, yet as only he and heaven knew, the adulterous passion that he held for his queen had tainted his heart and his soul, making him unworthy to receive the Grail. Percival came closest of all the other misfortunate knights. Brave, chaste and true, he was one of the finest knights in the world, yet a dark and distant place in his heart caused him to lack the courage to recognize the Holy Grail when it was brought before him. In defeat, he rode back toward Camelot to report his failure.

On his way, Percival met up with Galahad and was amazed at what the young knight had achieved. Galahad was dressed in pure gold armor that shimmered like satin in the sun. On his arm he wore the white shield upon which Joseph of Aramathia used his own blood to paint a bold cross. Galahad set off alone upon his quest, but he was now glad to have Percival to keep him company.

The knights rode together and ventured to the sea, where they found a lovely maiden who beckoned them into an awaiting boat. The beauty of the young girl's face and the serenity of her blue eyes radiated a feeling of calm and peace, and so Galahad and Percival boarded the small vessel.

The first days of the voyage went smoothly upon the soft rolling sea, but on the third day the heat of the sun became almost unbearable. The two knights removed their armor to keep from being baked alive. The maiden became sick with a high fever. A storm raged across the foaming sea on the fourth day, tossing the small vessel recklessly from one wave to another. The knights were powerless against the angry force of the world, and even more helpless as they watched their lovely companion die before them. Galahad and Percival said prayers as they wrapped the maiden in a cloak and buried her at sea.

On the fifth day, with calm weather and a golden sun, the small craft ran ashore. Galahad spied a small hovel in the shadows of the forest that bordered the beach, and he and Percival went forward to discover who lived there. They received no answer to their knock at the door, but the door was open and they entered. Before them, upon a wooden throne shrouded with dust and wrapped in spider webs, sat the maimed king. He welcomed the knights with frail, open arms.

"It is good for you to come," the king said in a soft, raspy voice. "This wound in my side will not heal and becomes worse everyday. The longer I remain ill, the more my kingdom becomes sickened and wasted. One of you can heal me, thus restoring my kingdom to its former grace and beauty. He who heals me will also find everlasting comfort in the Holy Grail."

As the king's voice dwindled into silence, a procession entered the small hovel: the young girl who had sailed upon the small boat with the knights; two young maidens who carried candles in their soft white hands; a maiden who carried a wooden crown wrapped in thorns upon a crimson pillow; and a maiden who carried a wooden chalice beneath a cover of shimmering white silk. The five maidens were dressed in blue, their faces beautiful and pleasant, though solemn and dedicated to their ritual. They stopped in front of Galahad. The knight dropped to his knees and offered a prayer for sight in front of him. In deep meditation, he stood and took the crown in his hands and placed it upon the king's head. Immediately, color returned to the king's shallow cheeks. The wound in his side healed, leaving no scar. The king stood from his throne and picked up the Grail. Galahad again dropped to his knees and offered a prayer, graciously accepting the offer to drink from the sacred chalice.

As he drank, Galahad saw wonders that he had only dreamed could be possible. The golden rays of the sun touched his shoulders and the young knight found himself standing among the clouds. A host of angels stood before him, singing the most beautiful music Galahad could ever hope to hear. The sky opened up to reveal a magnificent procession that captured the young knight's heart for all eternity. Galahad took the Holy Grail in his hands, stepped to the front of the procession and led the heavenly host on beyond the clouds.

Percival stood in the hovel alone, amazed at the sight that unfolded before him. He remained on the beach for several days, kneeling in the sand and offering prayers to the heavens, and then set off for Camelot to tell of the miracle which he had witnessed. Turning to leave the vacant hovel, he glanced back toward the sky and offered a last farewell to his noble companion — Galahad, the knight who won the Holy Grail.

Sir Galahad

Sir Lancelot's Armour

Historical Merlin

Two Merlins appear in the medieval histories of England under the names Emrys and Myrddin. Neither man lived during the time of Arthur, yet both men share near-identical physical and psychological profiles.

The first Merlin, it appears, lived during the reign of Vortigern and the early years of Ambrosius. He died 25 years before any historical mention of Arthur but because of royal, or near-royal bloodlines, the two may have been related. Historical records indicate that Merlin may have been a prince and superintended several kingdoms within Vortigern's dominion. He was a mighty warrior, a large man who swung his sword with impressive power and accuracy.

We may never fully separate fact from fiction, but the early writings about Merlin suggest that he employed his good looks to seduce women and that he was romantically involved with Queen Muirgen (Morgan le Fay) of Gore and then later with Vivien, the Lady of the Lake.

Two accounts concerning his prophetic ability exist, but both are fragmented and hard to decipher. One version claims that during the course of battle, Merlin witnessed the slaughter of his family and became psychologically unbalanced; the result was a gift of prophetic sight. The other version claims that Merlin was born under supernatural conditions and thus received his prophetic gift at birth. Modern historians believe that Merlin was thought to have had prophetic abilities because of his involvement in medieval science and his druidic association, a politically powerful religious confederation of Celtic priests and medicine men. The name Myrddin was a title associated with prophecy and mysticism.

The second Merlin, who appears to have lived after Arthur's death, was also a large man and a great warrior. Historical records suggest that he, too, was a womanizer, though no mention is made of any particular women. He is referred to as the "Wild Poet of Celidonius," and is said to have gone crazy during a battle because of blood-guilt, a suggestion that he breached a taboo by killing a blood relation. In his madness, Merlin received the gift of prophetic sight and fled into the woods where he spent his time upon a rock in the middle of Stream Mellodonor, interrupting the religious services of St. Kentigern's clergy by shouting out prophecies. Geoffrey of Monmouth edited and transposed a lengthy medieval manuscript and claimed it to be a collection of Merlin's prophecies concerning the fate of Breton.

Merlin died on the banks of an unknown river during a battle. According to historical records, the battle was not against invading Saxons, but between rival Breton clans.

The Merlin of the Authurian Romances seems to be a combination of the two Merlins. The legends and folklore adopted the earlier Merlin's abilities as a political and warfare strategist and embellished upon the later Merlin's wild nature and prophetic gift. However, though both Merlins spent a lot of time in the battlefields, the legends do not describe or depict the Merlin of the romances as a warrior. The Merlin with whom we have become familiar is a cunning, crafty and intelligent man who operated his magic within cover of the shadows.

Historical Arthur

Scholars and historians debate continually over the exact dates and places associated with the reign of King Arthur, and some even doubt the actual existence of England's most famous king. The truth about Arthur may always remain obscured by the folklore and legends that surround him because the majority of medieval historical records contemporary to Arthur's time are fragmented, and because medieval historians spend more time embellishing their writings with tales of the fantastic rather than the facts. Several dates and places concerning Arthur have been substantiated, however, and through bits and pieces of medieval transcripts we can reconstruct a picture of Arthur that doubting scholars cannot disprove.

One of the earliest historical mentions of Arthur comes from a monk (or a collection of monks) named Nennius. In his "Historia Brittonum," Nennius speaks of an Arthur who fought and won 12 battles against the Saxons, including a battle at Badon Hill where Arthur killed 960 men with his own hand and drove the Teutonic invaders out of Briton. Gildas, another historian who was a contemporary of Arthur's, fails to mention the king at all, but researchers and historians have concluded that the account by Gildas is not reliable because of the fanatical political/religious bent of his writings that lashed out at the wretched Britons for not embracing the religious doctrines of Rome. It is believed that Gildas omitted particular people from his history because of their religion. Arthur, though he carried a shield emblazoned with a figure of the Virgin Mary into battle, did not wholly adopt Christianity and often sided with the old religion that was regaining popularity at the time. It also seems that Arthur killed a relative of Gildas, perhaps another reason why Gildas omitted Arthur from the history.

From other historical fragments, though, Arthur has been traced to the late fifth and early sixth centuries. His Roman name was Artorius, and he was a cavalry commander under the Roman commander Ambrosius Aurelianus, the last of the Roman kings to remain in Britain. The Roman Empire was disintegrating and no longer offered the Britons protection from their Teutonic invaders. The country was divided into a confederation of numerous kingdoms, and it is speculated that Arthur, who time and again is referred to in historical records as a shrewd and cunning warrior, was commissioned by Ambrosius to rove Britain and assist the various kings in their battles against Teutonic invaders. Due to his success in driving out the Saxons and pushing the Picts and the Scots back into the highlands, Arthur became a figure greatly esteemed by his countrymen and since there was a tendency to acknowledge particularly powerful people as the single overlord of all the kingdoms, Arthur was probably designated as the successor to Ambrosius.

Changes in medieval leadership often raised questions of alliances and land ownership, which were usually decided by warfare. Historical records indicate that Arthur was successful in quelling assaults against his leadership and enjoyed peace and prosperity during his reign over Briton.

Arthur and Guinevere's Court Clothes